Vegan]
Cookbook

Delicious Vegan Recipes for Breakfast

Copyright 2018 by Grizzly Publishing - All rights reserved.

This document is geared towards providing exact and reliable information in regards to the topic and issue covered. The publication is sold with the idea that the publisher is not required to render an accounting, officially permitted, or otherwise, qualified services. If advice is necessary, legal or professional, a practiced individual in the profession should be ordered.

- From a Declaration of Principles which was accepted and approved equally by a Committee of the American Bar Association and a Committee of Publishers and Associations.

In no way is it legal to reproduce, duplicate, or transmit any part of this document in either electronic means or in printed format. Recording of this publication is strictly prohibited and any storage of this document is not allowed unless with written permission from the publisher. All rights reserved.

The information provided herein is stated to be truthful and consistent, in that any liability, in terms of inattention or otherwise, by any usage or abuse of any policies, processes, or directions contained within is the solitary and utter responsibility of the recipient reader. Under no circumstances will any legal responsibility or blame be held against the publisher for any reparation, damages, or monetary loss due to the information herein, either directly or indirectly.

Respective authors own all copyrights not held by the publisher.

The information herein is offered for informational purposes solely and is universal as so. The presentation of the information is without a contract or any type of guarantee assurance.

The trademarks that are used are without any consent, and the publication of the trademark is without permission or backing by the trademark owner. All trademarks and brands within this book are for clarifying purposes only and are the owned by the owners themselves, not affiliated with this document.

www.grizzlypublishing.com

Introduction

I want to thank you for purchasing this book, *"Vegan Breakfast Cookbook: Delicious Vegan recipes for Breakfast."*

Vegan diet has become quite popular nowadays. The word *Vegan* still continues to attract cynical eyebrow-raises and blank stares from people who are not entirely aware of the concept or what it actually means. Few people think that *vegan* is a short-form for *vegetarian* while there are others who believe that a vegan diet means that you can only eat salads as all three meals in a day.

Veganism is a cruelty-free way of living where you eliminate all forms of animal cruelty and exploitation from your daily life – be it for food, luxury, cosmetics, clothing or any other use. This also includes medication and entertainment options that exploit animals. It is for these reasons a vegan diet doesn't contain any animal products such as dairy, meat, honey and eggs.

Most people choose to go vegan for the environment and ethical reasons, but a considerate number of people choose veganism for the health benefits it entails. The ultimate desire to be healthy and disease-free encourages them to switch to a plant-based diet. When you follow a proper healthy vegan diet plan, you enjoy several health benefits, which include improved blood sugar control and a trim waistline!

The majority of the population is used to the preconceived notion that milk and meat are critical elements of a healthy diet. But this is not true! A properly planned vegan diet has all the required nutrients your body needs and follows healthy and well-balanced eating guidelines. The American Academy of Nutrition and Dietetics and the British Dietetic Association confirms that vegan dietary approach is suitable for all age groups at every stage of life. Eating a completely plant-based diet supports good health and protects the planet and helps the voiceless (animals).

When you decide to go vegan, you create an opportunity for yourself to learn more about your diet by learning more about nutritional facts and of course – cooking! The World Health Organization (WHO) has already classified processed meat as one of the causes of cancer. Going vegan naturally eliminates the risk of severe and deadly diseases, as you won't consume eggs, milk, processed meat and saturated fat (from meat). This means you don't consume too many calories, which will take care of the weight issues. You eat a more health-friendly diet as you get all your nutrients from plant-based foods.

If you are ready to make smart choices like eating plenty of vegetables, nuts, fruit, seeds, whole grains while limiting salt and sugar (refined and unrefined), you habituate yourself into a healthy eating style.

A vegan dietary pattern doesn't include meat, poultry, seafood, fish, dairy, bee products, eggs and any animal-based ingredients (gelatin, whey, etc.). It is also possible to substitute the animal products with plant-based replacements such as,

- Seitan, Tofu and Tempeh (protein-rich alternative to eggs, fish, meat and poultry)
- Legumes (a rich source of nutrients)

- Nut butters and nuts (best sources of zinc, vitamin E, fiber, selenium, iron and magnesium)
- Seeds like flax, chia and hemp are rich in omega-3 fatty acids (also protein-rich)
- Plant-based milks and yogurts (alternative for dairy. You can also add calcium-fortified plant yogurts and milks)
- Chlorella and Spirulina (rich iodine and protein sources)
- Nutritional yeast (use vitamin B12 fortified often)
- Cereals, whole grains and pseudo-cereals (rich sources of vitamin B, fiber, complex carbs, iron, several minerals and high-protein)
- Sprouted and fermented foods like pickles, miso, kimchi, tempeh, Ezekiel bread, sauerkraut, kombucha and natto (minerals, vitamin K2 and probiotics)
- Vegetables and Fruit (calcium, iron and several other nutrients)

Eating real and wholesome plant-based food helps in improving your health by lowering blood pressure, cholesterol, Type 2 diabetes, heart disease risks and specific cancer types over time. You also get to gain few other benefits such as improved digestion, loss of weight, low inflammation, longevity, clear skin and better sleep patterns.

How does a vegan diet contribute to weight loss? People consume fewer calories as their dietary fiber intake is more which gives them the satiated feeling.

The vegan diet is economical and easy on your pocket if you consume seasonal and local produce from your local organic farmers' market. Therefore, filling your plate with healthy plant-based food is more beneficial to your health when compared to the animal-based diet, which often leaves you bloated, sleepy and lethargic, as these foods are mostly acidic in nature.

As you know that breakfast is the most important meal of the day. So this book is a treasure trove for vegans who are looking for a nutritious breakfast option. It is quite easy to prepare a wholesome vegan breakfast meal as most of them are simple and easy-to-cook. The vegan recipes mentioned in the book are amazingly healthy and easy to make. Most of them have ingredients that carry the required phytochemicals (plant nutrients) that are essential for your body.

I hope this book serves as an informative and interesting read to you!

Thanks again for purchasing this book. I hope you enjoy it!

Chapter One: Vegan Breakfast Smoothie Recipes

Enlighten Smoothie Bowl

Servings: 1

Ingredients:

For the smoothie mix

- 1 1/2 fresh banana (or frozen; other half for topping)
- 2 tablespoons almond butter
- 1 1/2 cups berry mix (or strawberry mix)
- 3 – 4 ice cubes
- 1/2 cup water

For toppings (use any or few of them)

- 1 teaspoon shredded coconut
- 1 teaspoon blueberries
- 1/2 teaspoon cacao nibs
- 2 sliced strawberries
- 1 sliced kiwi
- 1 teaspoon hemp hearts
- 1 teaspoon almonds
- 1/2 teaspoon chia seeds

Method:

1. Add banana, almond butter, berry mix and water in a high-speed blender.
2. Blend on high for 30 seconds until smooth.

3. Add the ice cubes and blend again until the smoothie gets a rich, creamy texture
4. Don't add the ice cubes if you are using frozen banana
5. Transfer to a bowl and top it with sliced frozen banana, shredded coconut and cacao nibs. (You can also try any combination of your choice from the toppings ingredients)
6. Serve chilled

Glow Smoothie Bowl

Servings: 2

Ingredients:

For the smoothie bowl:

- 1/3 cup avocado (packed)
- 1 cup fresh baby spinach (packed)
- 1 heaping cup mango chunks (frozen)
- 1/2-inch piece ginger (peeled)
- 1/4 cup Medjool dates (pitted)
- 3 ice cubes
- 1 small peeled clementine
- 3/4 cup water
- 1/2 teaspoon matcha green tea powder

For the toppings:

- Raspberries, strawberries, blueberries
- Chopped and segmented Clementines
- Fresh mango (Diced)
- Hemp hearts
- Vanilla Super Seed Granola

Method:

1. Add avocado, baby spinach, mango, ginger, dates, Clementine along with water into a high-speed blender.
2. Blend until smooth on high
3. Add the ice cubes and matcha green tea powder to the mixture. Blend again until smooth

4. Transfer the smoothie into a bowl and add the toppings (you can add all or the ones you desire)
5. Serve cold. Enjoy!

Glow Green Smoothie

Servings: 5

Ingredients:

- 1/2 cup mango chunks (frozen)
- 2/3 cup fresh parsley leaves (loosely packed)
- 1/4 cup avocado (packed)
- 2 large cored and chopped Granny Smith apples
- 2 cups romaine or red leaf lettuce (packed)
- 1/3 cup fresh cilantro leaves (packed)
- 2 small fresh turmeric (peeled pinky-sized pieces)
- 1/2 cup mango juice (organic)
- 1 cup coconut water
- 5 to 6 ice cubes (large)
- 4 teaspoons fresh lemon juice

Method:

1. Take a 64-ounce high-speed blender and add mango juice and coconut water into it.
2. Also, add the mango, parsley, avocado, apples, romaine, cilantro and turmeric into the blender.
3. Blend on high until smooth. Add the lemon juice and ice cubes into the mixture.
4. Blend again until super smooth. Taste and add liquid sweetener if is too tart.
5. Transfer the smoothie to a glass.
6. Serve cold!

5-Minute Breakfast Smoothie

Serves: 1

Ingredients:

- 1 sliced ripe banana
- 1 cup fruit medley (pineapple, strawberry, papaya, mango) – all frozen
- 1 cup almond milk
- 2 tablespoons chia seeds
- 1 tablespoon coconut oil
- 1 teaspoon ginger (powdered)

Method:

1. Add the banana, frozen fruits, almond milk, chia seeds and ginger into a high-speed blender.
2. Blend for 30 seconds on high speed until smooth
3. Add the coconut oil.
4. Blend again on high for 60 seconds until creamy and smooth
5. Transfer to a glass and serve chilled.

Creamy Vegan Breakfast Smoothie

Serves: 1

Ingredients:

- 1/2 cup blackberries (frozen)
- 1 banana (large)
- 5.3 ounce Silk Dairy-Free Yogurt Alternative (Black Cherry flavor) – 1 container
- 4 ounces Silk Original Soy Creamer

Method:

1. Add the blackberries, banana, yogurt and soy creamer into a high-speed blender
2. Blend on high for 30 seconds until creamy and smooth
3. Transfer to a glass and serve chilled

Oatmeal and Strawberry Smoothie

Servings: 2

Ingredients:

- 14 strawberries (frozen)
- 1 banana, peeled and sliced
- 1/2 cup rolled oats
- 1 cup almond milk
- 1/2 teaspoon vanilla extract
- 1 1/2 teaspoons agave nectar (optional)

Method:

1. Add the strawberries, oats, banana chunks, almond milk and vanilla extract into a high speed blender
2. Blend on high for 30 seconds until smooth
3. Add agave nectar (if you want more sweetness to your smoothie) and blend again until creamy and smooth
4. Transfer to a glass and serve chilled

Mystic Mango Smoothie

Servings: 4

Ingredients:

- 2 cups mango (frozen)
- 1/4 cup avocado
- 1/2 teaspoon lime zest (finely grated)
- 1/2 cup water
- 1.5 cups orange juice
- 1 teaspoon pure maple syrup

Method:

1. Add the mango, avocado, lime zest, orange juice and water into a high-speed blender.
2. Blend on high for 60 seconds until creamy and smooth
3. Add the maple syrup and a bit of water (if the texture is too thick) into the mixture.
4. Blend again on high until smooth.
5. Transfer to a glass and serve cold.

Happy Digestion Smoothie

Servings: 2

Ingredients:

- 1 heaping cup pineapple chunks (frozen)
- 1 teaspoon packed ginger (fresh grated)
- 1/2 large banana (frozen)
- 1/4 cup fresh parsley leaves (packed)
- 2 tablespoons avocado
- 1/2 cup water
- 1/2 cup coconut water
- Lemon or lime slice (for garnishing)

Method:

1. Pour water and coconut water into a high-speed blender.
2. Now, add the pineapple, ginger, banana, parsley and avocado into the blender
3. Blend on high speed for 60 seconds until creamy and smooth
4. Transfer into a glass, add 2 ice cubes and insert the lime slice to the outline of the glass
5. Serve cold.

Banana Oat Smoothie

Servings: 1

Ingredients:

- 1 medium-sized frozen ripe banana,
- 1/4 cup rolled oats
- 1/4 cup almond milk (unsweetened)
- 1 tablespoon chia seeds
- 1/2 cup non-dairy yogurt (coconut or soy)
- 1/2 teaspoon vanilla extract
- 2 teaspoon maple syrup
- Pinch of salt

Method:

1. Add the banana, oats, almond milk, chia seeds and vanilla extract into a high-speed blender
2. Blend on high for 60 seconds until smooth
3. Add the salt and maple syrup into the mixture. Blend again until the chia seeds have completely broken down.
4. Transfer to the glass when you achieve the creamy-smooth texture. Serve cold.
5. You can also refrigerate the smoothie overnight to get a more thick texture. Add a bit of almond milk while serving the next day.

Banana Mango Smoothie

Servings: 2

Ingredients:

- 1 banana (large)
- 1 cup mango (frozen)
- 1/2 cup coconut milk (or almond milk)
- 1/2 cup orange juice (organic)
- 1 tablespoon chia seeds
- 2 drops Lemon or Orange essential oil

Method:

1. Add the banana, mango, chia seeds and coconut milk into the high-speed blender.
2. Blend on high until smooth.
3. Now, add the orange juice and essential oil into the mixture.
4. Blend again on high until the chia seeds completely break down
5. Transfer to a glass and serve chilled.

Rise and Shine smoothie

Servings: 2

Ingredients:

- 1 banana (frozen)
- 3 small dried Medjool dates (pitted)
- 1/2 cup coconut water
- 2 tablespoons almond butter (unsalted and unsweetened)
- 1 cup almond milk (unsweetened)
- 2 tablespoons + small sprinkling hemp seeds
- Pinch of cinnamon (ground)

Method:

1. Add the banana, dates, coconut water, almond butter and hemp seeds into a high-speed blender.
2. Blend on high for 30 seconds. Now, add the almond milk to the mixture and blend again for 60 seconds until smooth.
3. Add cinnamon and blend once more until the smoothie reaches a creamy consistency.
4. Transfer it to a glass and sprinkle the hemp seeds on the top
5. Serve cold.

Chocolate chip power bomb smoothie

Servings: 2

Ingredients:

- 1 1/2 bananas (frozen)
- 1 medjool dates (pitted)
- 1 tablespoon almond butter
- 1 cup almond milk (unsweetened)
- 1 tablespoon chia seeds
- 2 tablespoons cacao nibs (raw)
- 1/2 cup coconut water
- 1 teaspoon maca powder
- 3 tablespoons hemp seeds
- 5 ice cubes

Method:

1. Add the bananas, dates, almond butter, almond milk, chia seeds, hemp seeds, cacao, coconut water and maca powder into a high-speed blender
2. Blend on high for 30 seconds.
3. Add the ice cubes to the mixture and blend again for 60 seconds until creamy and smooth
4. Transfer into a glass and serve chilled.

Apple pie green smoothie

Servings: 2

Ingredients:

- 2 cups spinach (fresh)
- 1 chopped and frozen apple
- 1/2 English cucumber
- 1/4 chopped and frozen avocado
- 1 tablespoon walnuts
- 1/2 cup apple juice (unsweetened unpasteurized)
- 1/4 teaspoon maple extract or vanilla extract
- Pinch nutmeg (ground)
- 1/2 teaspoon cinnamon (ground)
- 1/2 cup water
- 4 ice cubes

Method:

1. Add the spinach, apple, cucumber, avocado, walnuts, apple juice, maple extract, nutmeg, cinnamon and water into the high-speed blender.
2. Blend on high for 30 seconds
3. Add the ice cubes into the mixture and blend again on high
4. Let it blend until the mixture reaches a creamy and smooth consistency
5. Transfer to a glass and serve cold

Strawberry Cheesecake Smoothie

Servings: 1

Ingredients:

- 1 cup strawberries
- 1 tablespoon chia seeds
- 1 cup unsweetened almond milk
- 1 tablespoon cashews
- 3 tablespoon oats (uncontaminated)
- 1 teaspoon lemon juice
- Pinch stevia
- 1 teaspoon apple cider vinegar
- 1/2 teaspoon vanilla

Method:

1. Pour the almond milk and lemon juice into a large glass container or Mason jar.
2. Add the strawberries, chia seeds, cashews, oats, stevia, apple cider vinegar and vanilla into the glass container.
3. Combine them together by stirring or give it a quick shake.
4. Refrigerate the contents overnight or for 4 hours
5. Transfer the contents of the container into a high-speed blender. Blend on high for 60 seconds until smooth and creamy
6. Top it with cashews and serve chilled.

Blueberry Muffin Smoothie

Servings: 1

Ingredients:

- 1/2 cup blueberries
- 1 1/2 cup almond or coconut milk
- 1 tablespoon vanilla protein powder
- 2 tablespoons regular oats (uncontaminated) or quinoa flakes
- 1 tablespoon chia seeds
- 1 teaspoon pure vanilla extract

Method:

1. Pour the almond milk into a large glass container or Mason jar.
2. Add the vanilla protein powder, quinoa flakes, chia seeds and pure vanilla extract into the glass container.
3. Combine them together by stirring or give it a quick shake.
4. Refrigerate the contents overnight or for 4 hours
5. Transfer the contents of the container into a high-speed blender. Add the blueberries now.
6. Blend on high for 60 seconds until smooth and creamy
7. Transfer to a glass and serve chilled

Energy smoothies

Servings: 1

Ingredients:

For Strawberry banana flavor

- 6 strawberries
- 1/2 banana
- 1 tablespoon chia seeds
- 1 cup green tea
- Probiotics (1 serving)
- 1 scoop protein powder

For Blueberry peach flavor

- 1 cup blueberries
- 1/2 peach
- 1 tablespoon chia seeds
- 1 cup green tea
- Probiotics (1 serving)
- 1 scoop protein powder

Method:

1. You can choose one flavor or prepare both.
2. Take 2 one-liter Mason jar and add the strawberry banana flavor ingredients in one and blueberry peach flavor ingredients in the other.
3. Combine the ingredients well by stirring or give it a shake.
4. Seal the jars and refrigerate overnight.

5. Transfer the contents of the strawberry banana flavor into a high-speed blender and blend on high for 60 seconds until creamy and smooth
6. Repeat step 5 for blueberry peach flavor
7. Transfer the smoothies into two different glasses
8. Serve chilled.
9. You can refrigerate the smoothies for 2 days (it stays well!)

Chocolate covered raspberry green smoothie

Servings: 1

Ingredients:

- 1 cup raspberries
- 2 tablespoon coconut flakes (shredded)
- 2 cups spinach (organic)
- 1 cup almond milk (unsweetened)
- 1 tablespoon cacao powder
- 2 tablespoon flax seed (ground)
- 3 ice cubes

Method:

1. Add the raspberries, coconut flakes, spinach, almond milk, cacao powder and flax seed into a high-speed blender.
2. Blend on high for 30 seconds until smooth
3. Add the ice cubes to the mixture and blend again on high.
4. Let it pulse until the texture is creamy and smooth
5. Transfer to a glass and serve chilled.

Chapter Two: Vegan Breakfast Dishes Recipes

Quinoa Bowl

Servings: 1

Ingredients:

- 1/2 cup quinoa (cooked)
- 1/2 cup grated carrot
- 1/2 cup crumbled tofu (extra firm)
- 1/4 cup sliced avocado
- 1/2 cup broccoli (chopped)
- 1/4 cup micro greens or deli sprouts
- 1/4 cup cherry tomatoes (sliced into half)
- 1 cup kale (chopped)
- 1/4 cup sliced mushrooms
- 1/4 teaspoon onion powder
- 1/2 teaspoon yellow curry powder
- 1/4 teaspoon paprika
- 1/8 teaspoon pepper
- 1/4 teaspoon garlic powder
- 1/4 teaspoon salt
- 1 lime (sliced into half)

Method:

1. Heat a saucepan at high heat.
2. Mix the onion powder, curry powder, paprika, garlic powder, pepper and salt in a small bowl
3. Add the carrots, broccoli and mushrooms to the heated saucepan. Splash some water over the

vegetables and cook for 4 minutes until they become soft and tender

4. Reduce the heat to medium and add the cherry tomatoes and kale. Continue to stir the contents.
5. Add the spice mix from the bowl and continue to sauté for few more minutes until the kale wilts
6. Add splashes of water to prevent the vegetables from sticking or getting burnt
7. Squeeze the lime juice into the pan and add the scrambled tofu.
8. Mix them with the vegetables until thoroughly combined. Keep stirring until the tofu turns light brown
9. Once the tofu is cooked well, transfer the contents into a bowl of cooked quinoa.
10. Top the mixture with sprouts and sliced avocado. Squeeze another lime (if needed), sprinkle some pepper and salt.
11. Serve hot.

Vegan burritos

Servings: 4

Ingredients:

For the Tofu Scramble

- 1 package crumbled pressed or extra-firm tofu
- 4 large white mushrooms (sliced)
- 1/4 heaping cup diced red onion
- 2 garlic cloves
- 1/2 teaspoon (each) chili powder, garlic powder, cumin, turmeric, salt and pepper mixed with 3 teaspoons of water (*the spice mixture*)
- 1/2 diced red bell pepper,

For the Burrito

- 1 Sliced avocado
- 2-3 Wraps
- 1 tablespoon Refried beans
- 1 tablespoon Fresh lime juice
- 2 tablespoons Fresh cilantro
- 2 tablespoons Salsa
- 1/4 cup Lettuce

Method:

1. Heat a pan (non-sticky) over medium heat.
2. Add the onion, mushrooms, garlic and red pepper and cook for 7 minutes until the mushrooms and onions begin to soften. Add a splash of water if required.
3. Add the spice mixture and crumbled tofu to the pan. Stir well until all the contents are combined.

4. Cook until the tofu turns light brown or is thoroughly heated. Set it aside once done
5. Take another small pan and heat up the refried beans (you can ignore this step if you like the beans cold)
6. Prepare the wraps by adding the lettuce, cilantro, salsa, beans, avocado and a large scoop of the tofu scramble.
7. Spray some lime juice and wrap it up
8. Serve warm

Vegan Chickpea Omelet

Servings: 2

Ingredients:

For the Chickpea batter:

- 3/4 cups chickpea flour
- 1/4 teaspoon garlic powder
- 3/4 cups + 1 tablespoon coconut milk (unsweetened)
- 1/4 teaspoon onion powder
- 2 teaspoons apple cider vinegar
- 1/4 teaspoon baking soda
- 1/4 teaspoon sea salt to taste
- 1/4 teaspoon turmeric powder
- 2 teaspoons nutritional yeast (optional)

For the Stuffing:

- 1/4 of a red onion (finely chopped)
- 1/4 cup chopped tomatoes
- 2 minced garlic cloves
- 1 tablespoon cilantro
- 1/4 cup broccoli florets (small)
- 1 teaspoon olive oil

Method:

1. Whisk the chickpea flour, garlic powder, coconut milk, onion powder, apple cider vinegar, baking soda, turmeric powder, nutritional yeast and salt together in a Pyrex measuring cup. The consistency shouldn't be too thick but like a pancake batter (easy-to-pour

consistency). Let the chickpea batter sit for some time.

2. Heat a nonstick skillet and sauté the garlic and green onion until they turn light brown. Add the broccoli and cook until the florets begin to soften. Transfer the contents to a plate and set aside

3. Add olive oil to the skillet (the same one) and pour half the batter into it.

4. Add the cooked mixture (garlic, green onion and broccoli) and tomatoes on top of the batter.

5. Let it cook for 2 minutes until the batter bubbles and begins to firm up along the edges.

6. When done, fold over to one side gently and let it cook for another minute.

7. Cover with a lid and turn off the stove. Allow it to steam for 5 minutes

8. Transfer to a plate and garnish with cilantro, sliced avocado, more tomatoes, red onion (minced) and lime wedges.

9. Sprinkle pepper and sea salt. Serve warm.

Vegan Egg breakfast

Servings: 8

Ingredients:

- 16 ounces extra firm or firm tofu (packed in water)
- 2 1/2 tablespoons Nutritional Yeast
- 1 1/4 teaspoon garlic (granulated)
- 2 tablespoons Vegan Margarine
- 1 1/4 teaspoon onion (granulated)
- 1/2 teaspoon black pepper
- 3/4 teaspoon pink Himalayan salt or sea salt
- 1/8 teaspoon turmeric
- Optional: ketchup, vegan cheese, black salt

Method:

1. Drain the water off the tofu
2. Heat a large skillet on medium heat and add the margarine. Crumble the tofu into the skillet and toss it with margarine
3. Sprinkle the garlic, onion, pepper, salt and turmeric over the tofu and mix until combined well
4. Cook on medium heat for 5 minutes as you keep stirring frequently to prevent sticking
5. Add the nutritional yeast when the water gets completely cooked out of the tofu.
6. Stir and continue to cook until the tofu turns brown.
7. Turn it over using a spatula and wait until the other side turns brown
8. Transfer to a plate and serve with ketchup, vegan cheese or black salt.

Vegan French toast

Servings: 3

Ingredients:

- 1 cup almond milk
- 6 slices (3/4 inch thick) ciabatta bread (one day old)
- 2 tablespoons millet or whole wheat or Spelt flour
- 1/4 teaspoon nutmeg (freshly ground)
- 1 tablespoon maple syrup
- 1 teaspoon cinnamon
- 1 tablespoon nutritional yeast
- 1 teaspoon coconut oil
- Pinch of salt

For Toppings:

- Fresh fruit
- Vegan butter
- Maple syrup
- Powdered sugar

Method:

1. Whisk the almond milk, flour, nutmeg, maple syrup, cinnamon, nutritional yeast and salt together in a small bowl
2. Take a shallow dish with sides and place the bread in it. Pour the whisked mixture over the bread and flip it over. Ensure both the sides are evenly coated. Repeat the process for all the bread slices.
3. Heat coconut oil in a large skillet over medium heat. Place the coated bread slices on the heated oil and cook for 2 minutes until it turns golden brown

4. Flip the side and cook for another minute.
5. Transfer to a serving plate and serve with fresh fruit, vegan butter, maple syrup and fresh fruit

Baked beans

Servings: 2

Ingredients:

- 8.4 ounces drained cannellini beans (1 tin has 14 ounces when drained it becomes 8.4 ounces)
- 1/2 onion (finely diced)
- 1 tablespoon tomato purée
- 1/2 cup passata
- 2 minced garlic cloves
- 1 tablespoon olive oil
- 1 tablespoon soy sauce
- 1/2 tablespoon smoked paprika
- 1 tablespoon brown sugar
- 1/4 tablespoon thyme (dried)
- Black pepper

Method:

1. Take a saucepan and heat the olive oil in medium heat. Add the garlic and onion to the heated oil and cook for 5 minutes until it turns translucent and soft.
2. Add the tomato puree, soy sauce, paprika, brown sugar and thyme into the saucepan. Cook for few more minutes.
3. Add the beans and passata to the mixture. Simmer for 5 minutes until the sauce thickens a bit and the mixture is piping hot.
4. Stir again until the flavor blends well. Season with black pepper generously (you don't need salt because of the soy sauce, but if you need it you can add).

5. Transfer the baked beans to a plate (you can serve warm on toast)

Black Eyed Peas - Sweet Potato Hash

Servings: 4

Ingredients:

- 2 cups sweet potato (peeled and cubed – 1 sweet potato should do)
- 1.5 cups salted black-eyed peas (cooked)
- 1/2 chopped onion (medium)
- 3 finely chopped garlic cloves
- 2 cups chopped baby greens (frozen baby spinach)
- 1/2 green chopped bell pepper (small)
- 1 teaspoon harissa spice blend or 3 teaspoons paste
- 1/2 teaspoon smoked paprika
- 2 teaspoons olive oil
- 1/2 teaspoon thyme
- Scallions or cilantro (for garnishing)
- 1 teaspoon lemon juice (for garnishing)
- 1 teaspoon ground cumin black pepper (for garnishing)
- 1/2 teaspoon salt

Method:

1. Heat oil in a skillet over medium heat and add garlic, onion and a pinch of salt to it.
2. Cook for 6 minutes until it turns translucent. Keep stirring occasionally
3. Add bell pepper, sweet potato, thyme, spice blend and 1/4-teaspoon salt to the skillet.
4. Toss it well until coated and cover the skillet. Cook for 3 minutes.

5. Add a splash of water and mix until combined. Cover and cook for another 10 minutes.
6. Stir occasionally to check if the sweet potatoes are cooked (soft). Cover and cook until it is done
7. Add the greens and black-eyed peas into the skillet and mix well until combined.
8. Cook on medium high for 2 more minutes. Taste and add more salt if required. Add a teaspoon of olive oil, black pepper, cumin, lemon and mix well
9. Remove from the heat. Garnish with cilantro or scallions.
10. Serve hot with garlic bread, tortillas or toasted bread.
11. It also goes well with a bowl of cooked grains, lettuce and a dressing.

Cheesy Potato Casserole

Servings: 8

Ingredients:

- 3 red or yellow potatoes (medium and diced)
- 2 tablespoons chopped parsley
- 1 finely chopped onion (medium)
- 4 links (14 ounces) vegan Italian sausage (crumbled or thinly sliced)
- 3 minced garlic cloves
- 1/2 teaspoon red pepper flakes
- 1 teaspoon olive oil
- Salt to taste

For the cheesy sauce:

- 3/4 cup soaked raw cashews in 1 1/2 cups water (to be soaked for 30 minutes)
- 1/4 cup nutritional yeast
- 2 teaspoons onion powder
- 1/2 teaspoon dry sage
- 1 teaspoon garlic powder
- Salt and ground black pepper to taste

Method:

1. Blend all the *cheesy sauce* ingredients in a high-speed blender until creamy and smooth. Set aside the sauce.
2. Take a microwave-safe dish and place the potatoes in it. Add a tablespoon of water and cover it. Nuke on high for 5 minutes until the potatoes become tender

3. Preheat the oven to 350 F
4. Heat oil in a large skillet and add onions, parsley and garlic to it. Sauté it for a while. Season with pepper and salt and sauté for 5 minutes over medium heat.
5. Keep stirring while you sauté until the onions are translucent and soft
6. Add the potatoes and sausage to the skillet and let it cook for about 5 minutes. Check the taste and add more salt or pepper if required
7. Transfer the mixture to a baking dish and pour the cheesy sauce on the top of potato sausage mixture.
8. Bake for 30 minutes until the top begins to turn light brown. Now, switch to the broil function on the oven and broil for 5 more minutes in the highest setting.
9. Wait until you see the golden brown spots appearing on the potatoes and cheesy sauce
10. Remove from the oven and garnish with more parsley (if you like).
11. Serve hot and enjoy!

Vegan Okonomiyaki

Servings: 3

Ingredients:

For the Pancakes:

- 3/4 cup carrots
- 1/2 cabbage head
- 1/2 bell pepper (red or green)
- 3/4 cup white flour (unbleached)
- 1/4 cup chickpea flour
- 2 tablespoons scallions
- 1 inch minced ginger
- 2 teaspoons rice vinegar
- 1 tablespoon soy sauce
- 1 tablespoon nutritional yeast
- 1/2 salt
- 1/4 teaspoon white pepper
- 4 tablespoons water
- 1/8 teaspoon black salt (optional)
- 1/2 teaspoon baking powder (optional)

For the easy Tonkatsu sauce:

- 1 tablespoon vegan Worcestershire sauce
- 1 tablespoon ketchup
- 3 teaspoons water
- 1/2 teaspoon sugar

Method:

1. Shred the carrots, cabbage and bell pepper. Mix them all with vinegar in a large bowl.

36

2. Sieve the white flour, chickpea flour and baking powder into the bowl. Mix well until it combines well with the shredded vegetables

3. Make a mix that can spread, add water only if needed as the shredded vegetable will leave enough water to make the mix into a paste.

4. Add the scallions, ginger, soy sauce, nutritional yeast, salt, pepper and pinch of black salt. Mix well until you get a paste that can spread in a pan.

5. Heat oil in a pan over medium heat. Spread the vegetable batter and even it out to 1/2-inch thickness.

6. Add a little more oil and let it cook for 7 minutes until it turns crispy or golden brown.

7. Flip to the other side and cook for 7 more minutes. You can add more oil to avoid stickiness.

8. When the pancakes are getting cooked, take another bowl. Add the vegan Worcestershire sauce, ketchup, sugar and water. Mix the ingredients well until combined thoroughly and set it aside.

9. Transfer the cooked pancake to a plate and serve with the Tonkatsu sauce.

10. You can also serve the pancake with pickled ginger or vegan mayo along with the sauce. Enjoy!

Vegan Chilaquiles with Chickpeas

Servings: 4

Ingredients:

For the chilaquiles:

- 1.5 cups cooked Chickpeas garbanzo beans
- 1 finely chopped onion (small)
- 1/3 cup carrots (chopped)
- 5 finely chopped garlic cloves
- 1.5 cups tortilla chips or 2 tortillas
- 1/2 teaspoon garlic powder
- 1/2 teaspoon paprika
- 1 teaspoon coriander (ground)
- 1/4 teaspoon cayenne
- 3/4 teaspoon cumin (ground)
- 1/4 teaspoon salt
- 1/2 teaspoon dried oregano
- 1 teaspoon olive or coconut oil
- 1 tablespoon chopped red onion, cilantro and lime juice (for garnishing)
- Pinch of cinnamon

For the red sauce:

- 1 tomato
- 1/4 cup tomato paste
- 1 chipotle pepper in adobo sauce
- 1 cup water or vegetable stock
- 1/3 teaspoon salt
- 1/2 teaspoon cumin (ground)

Method:

1. Heat oil over medium heat in a large skillet. Add the carrots, onion, garlic and pinch of salt to the heated oil.

2. Cook for 6 minutes until it turns golden, keep stirring occasionally. Reserve half the mixture for the red sauce.

3. Add the chickpeas to the mixture in the skillet and stir while you add garlic powder, paprika, coriander, cayenne, cumin, oregano and salt. Mix well until combined.

4. Cover and cook for 5 minutes.

5. When it cooks, make the red sauce by blending all the red sauce ingredients and the reserved onion-garlic-carrot mixture in a high-speed blender.

6. Blend until it becomes smooth and set aside the sauce

7. Add the sliced tortilla to the skillet and pour the blended red sauce over them. Mix well and bring to boil. Taste and add more salt if required. Mix well until the contents are combined well.

8. Transfer to a plate and garnish with chopped onion, cilantro and lime juice.

9. Serve hot.

Lentil Veggie Asparagus Frittata

Servings: 4

Ingredients:

For the lentil mix:

- 1/2 cup split red lentils
- 1/4 cup almond meal
- 2 teaspoons arrowroot starch or cornstarch
- 1/2 teaspoon garlic paste
- 1 tablespoon chia seed meal or flaxseed meal
- 1/4 teaspoon turmeric + 1/8 teaspoon black pepper powder
- 1 teaspoon baking powder
- 1/3 teaspoon chipotle pepper powder + cayenne
- 2 teaspoons sun-dried tomatoes
- 2 tablespoons nutritional yeast
- 2 teaspoons extra virgin olive oil
- 1 teaspoon lemon juice
- 2/3 teaspoon salt
- 1 cup water

For the veggies:

- 2 cups chopped veggies (1 cup cauliflower small florets +1/2 cup chopped carrots + 1 tablespoon red bell pepper + 2 tablespoon peas + 1/2 cup mushrooms)
- 1/2 cup spinach + 1/4 cup celery leaves + 1/4 cup chopped cilantro (packed)
- 1/2 cup onion (chopped)
- 3 garlic cloves (large)

- 1/4 teaspoon oregano +1/4 teaspoon thyme
- 1 cup chopped asparagus (packed; should be easy-to-bite sizes)
- 1/3 teaspoon chipotle pepper powder + a dash of black pepper
- 1/3 teaspoon salt
- 1 teaspoon oil

Method:

1. Let the lentils soak in hot water for 20 minutes before you get started.
2. Preheat the oven to 365F. Grease the pan well and keep it ready

Veggie mixture

1. Heat oil in a large skillet over medium heat and add the onions and garlic to the heated oil.
2. Cook for 4 minutes until the onions turn translucent. Add the asparagus to the skillet and stir until it mixes well.
3. Now add the chopped vegetables and mix well. Cover and cook for about 2 minutes.
4. Add garlic, oregano, thyme, chipotle pepper, black pepper and salt to the veggies.
5. Mix well as you add the spinach. Cover and cook for 4 minutes until the spinach wilts. You can add a splash of water for the veggies to cook faster.
6. Remove from heat and let it sit for some time

Lentil mix

1. Drain the lentils from hot water and place it in a high-speed blender. Add one cup of water and blend for 1 minute.
2. Add the remaining ingredients from the *lentil ingredients section* to the blender and blend for 3 minutes until the mixture forms a smooth and creamy consistency
3. Transfer the cooked veggies to the greased pan and pour the lentil mixture little by little over the veggies. Spread with a spatula and tap for the mixture to settle in the veggies
4. Bake for 50 minutes until a toothpick comes out clean from the center (it shouldn't be wet when pricked)
5. Cool for 10 minutes and then again in the cooling rack for 10 more minutes
6. Slice and transfer to a plate. Serve immediately. You can dress it up with sauce if required

Turmeric Steel Cut Oats

Servings: 2

Ingredients:

- 1/2 cup steel cut oats
- 1/3 teaspoon turmeric
- 1 cup coconut or almond milk
- 1/2 teaspoon cinnamon
- 2 cups water
- 1/4 teaspoon cardamom
- 1/4 teaspoon oil
- 1/8 teaspoon salt
- 2 tablespoons maple syrup.

Method:

1. Toast the oats in heated oil in a saucepan over medium heat for 2 minutes until fragrant
2. Add the coconut milk and water to the saucepan and bring it to boil for about 5 minutes
3. Mix well and reduce the heat to medium-low. Keep stirring and let it cook for another 10 minutes
4. Add turmeric, cinnamon, cardamom and oil to the oats and mix well. Add the maple syrup and cook for 7 minutes until you can see a thick creamy consistency
5. If you want the sweet flavor to be less, you can add 2 teaspoons instead of a tablespoon and add pepper to the mixture.
6. Cook for few more minutes and let it cool for 5 minutes (this thickens the mixture further)
7. Transfer to a bowl and serve warm. You can garnish with chia seeds or dry fruits if required

Chipotle Roasted Corn Avocado Toast

Servings: 2

Ingredients:

For the roasted corn:

- 1 cup frozen corn or 2 medium ears of corn
- 1/2 teaspoon smoked paprika
- 1/2 teaspoon chipotle pepper powder
- 1/4 teaspoon salt
- 1/4 teaspoon black pepper

For the toast:

- Ciabatta slices or Multigrain bread
- 1/4 cup onion (finely chopped)
- 2 mashed avocados (ripe ones)
- Lemon juice to taste
- 1/4 cup cilantro (chopped)

Method:

Corn roast

1. Take a heavy bottom skillet and add the frozen corn kernels. Cook over high heat for 8 minutes until the kernels turn brown. Keep stirring occasionally to prevent the corn from getting burnt.
2. Add paprika, pepper, black pepper and salt to the corn. Mix well until well coated. Cook for another minute more until you get the roasted smell of the spices

Toast

1. Toast the ciabatta slices lightly and add a layer of mashed avocado on it.
2. Add the smoky roasted corn as the next layer and sprinkle the chopped onions and cilantro onto it
3. Spray the lime juice and add a pinch of salt. Serve immediately.

Chapter Three: Vegan Brunch Recipes

Ultimate Tofu Burrito Bowls

Servings: 3

Ingredients:

- 14 ounces drained extra-firm tofu
- 2 seeded and chopped jalapeno peppers
- 3 minced garlic cloves
- 2 cups tomatoes (chopped)
- 1 cup red onion (finely diced)
- 15.5 ounces drained and rinsed unsalted black beans (1 can)
- 1 1/2 cups hash brown potatoes (cooked)
- 1/4 cup fresh cilantro (chopped)
- 1 peeled, pitted and sliced avocado
- 1/2 teaspoon turmeric (ground)
- 1 1/2 teaspoons garlic powder
- 1 1/2 teaspoons cumin
- 1 1/2 teaspoons onion powder
- 1/4 cup fresh cilantro (chopped)
- 2 tablespoons fresh lemon juice
- 1 teaspoons hot sauce
- 3 tablespoons olive oil, divided
- 1/2 teaspoon salt
- Black pepper to taste

Method:

1. Preheat heavy skillet (large) over medium-high heat and add 2 tablespoons of olive oil.

2. Break the tofu into bite-size pieces and add it to the heated oil. Sprinkle the tofu with salt and pepper and cook as you keep stirring frequently.
3. Cook for 10 minutes until the tofu browns and liquid cooks out. Increase to high heat and stir continuously.
4. Scrape the bottom, as the tofu turns crispy to prevent it from sticking.
5. Now, add the garlic powder, turmeric, onion powder, lemon juice and the remaining oil to the skillet. Toss it and coat well and continue to cook for 5 more minutes
6. Preheat a heavy-bottomed saucepan and add oil. Cook the jalapeno, oil and a pinch of salt over medium-high heat. Add the garlic and stir the contents as you cook for another 30 seconds until the flavor turns aromatic.
7. Add tomatoes, cumin and salt and continue to cook for 5 minutes until the tomatoes get a saucy texture. Now, add the lime juice and cilantro and stir until combined well.
8. Continue to cook until the cilantro wilts and then add the beans as you stir the contents. Cook for 2 more minutes and taste. Add more salt if required.
9. Take a bowl and fill it with a spoon of hash browns followed by a scoop of beans and then a scoop of tofu scramble. Top it with avocado, a sprinkle of cilantro and lemon juice.
10. Serve with the hot sauce. Enjoy!

Tofu Quiche

Servings: 8

Ingredients:

- 1 1/2 pounds cubed extra-firm tofu
- 1 chopped medium sweet onion
- 8 ounces thinly sliced fresh spinach (like strips)
- 9 inches vegan pie crust (1)
- 8 ounces fresh mushrooms (sliced)
- 1/8 cup vegetable oil
- 1/4 cup red wine
- 1 minced garlic clove
- 1/4 cup Dijon mustard
- 2 tablespoons balsamic vinegar
- 1/4 cup arrowroot
- 1 teaspoon liquid smoke
- 1/4 cup olive oil
- 1/4 cup nutritional yeast
- 2 teaspoons agar-agar powder

Method:

1. Take a large pot and heat the vegetable oil over medium-high heat.
2. Sauté the onion in the heated oil for 5 minutes and add garlic and mushrooms. Cook for another 5 minutes as you keep stirring at constant intervals. Keep the pot covered between the stirs.
3. Add spinach, liquid smoke and balsamic vinegar to the pot. Stir for few seconds, cover the pot and remove from the heat. Let it cool.

4. Preheat the oven to 350 F and arrange the piecrust in a 10-inch pie plate.
5. Blend the tofu, olive oil, agar-agar powder, arrowroot and nutritional yeast in a food processor until it forms a thick paste.
6. Add this tofu mixture into the cooked mushroom mixture in the pot and mix well. This will form a more liquid paste. Scrape this mixture and pour it into the pie crust
7. Bake in the oven for 45 minutes until the crust turns golden and the center part is set. Cool the quiche completely. Slice it and serve immediately.

Country Style Fried Potatoes

Servings: 6

Ingredients:

- 6 large peeled and cubed potatoes
- 1/3 cup vegan shortening
- 1/2 teaspoon garlic powder
- 1/2 teaspoon paprika
- 1/2 teaspoon black pepper (ground)
- 1 teaspoon salt

Method:

1. Heat the vegan shortening in a large cast iron skillet over medium-high heat
2. Add the potatoes into the skillet and cook until they turn golden brown
3. Keep stirring as they get cooked.
4. Add the garlic powder, paprika, black pepper and salt when the potatoes turn brown.
5. Mix until the spices blend well. Transfer to a plate.
6. Serve hot.

Tofu Quiche with Broccoli

Servings: 6

Ingredients:

- 1 pound drained firm tofu
- 1 pound chopped broccoli
- 1 finely chopped onion
- 1/8 cup soy cheese (Parmesan flavor)
- 1 unbaked pie crust (9 inches)
- 4 minced garlic cloves
- 1/4 teaspoon Dijon mustard
- 1/2 teaspoon red pepper (ground)
- 1/2 cup soy milk
- 1 tablespoon dried parsley
- 1/4 teaspoon ground nutmeg
- 1 tablespoon olive oil
- 3/4 teaspoon salt
- Black pepper to taste

Method:

1. Preheat the oven to 400 F and bake the pie crust in the preheated oven for 12 minutes
2. Steam the broccoli over 1 inch of boiling water in a steamer. Cover and let it cook for 6 minutes until the broccoli is tender but still firm. Drain and keep it aside.
3. Heat oil in a large skillet and add the onion and garlic to the heated oil. Sauté them over medium-high heat until they turn golden.
4. Add the cooked broccoli and stir well until the contents are mixed. Heat through them.

5. Blend the tofu, mustard, nutmeg, black pepper, Parmesan soy cheese, soymilk, parsley, ground red pepper and salt until smooth.
6. Take a large bowl and combine the broccoli mixture with the tofu mixture. Make sure they are combined well.
7. Pour this into the piecrust and bake it in a preheated oven for 40 minutes until the quiche is set.
8. Let it stand for 5 minutes and slice the quiche. Serve warm.

Fava Bean Spread

Servings: 6

Ingredients:

- 15 ounces fava beans (1 can)
- 1 chopped large onion
- 1/4 cup fresh parsley (chopped)
- 1 diced large tomato
- 1 teaspoon cumin (ground)
- 1/4 cup fresh lemon juice
- 1 1/2 tablespoons olive oil
- 1 teaspoon red pepper (ground)
- Salt and black pepper to taste
- Grilled pita (2 or as per your need)

Method:

1. Pour the can of fava beans into a pot and bring it to boil. Keep stirring occasionally.
2. Add the onion, parsley, tomato, cumin, lemon juice, olive oil, red pepper and salt into the pot. Mix them well and bring it to boil again
3. Reduce the heat to medium and sprinkle black pepper and let the mixture cook for 5 more minutes
4. Transfer to a plate and serve with grilled pita. Enjoy!

Chickpea and onion omelet

Servings: 2

Ingredients:

- 1 medium onion (thinly sliced)
- 3 heaping tablespoons chickpea flour
- 1 tablespoon chopped dill
- 1 tablespoon chopped spring onions
- 1 tablespoon finely chopped basil
- 2 tablespoons oil
- 8 tablespoons water
- Pinch of black pepper (ground)
- 1/2 teaspoon salt

Method:

1. Add the chickpea flour, pepper and salt in a bowl and mix well until combined
2. Add water and continue to whisk until you get a creamy texture (batter)
3. Add the onions, dill, spring onions and basil to the batter and mix again until all the herbs blend well with the batter
4. Heat a frying pan over medium heat and add oil to it.
5. Scoop the batter onto the pan on the heated oil and spread it out using a spatula
6. Make the spread look like a nice big omelet. Let it cook for 2 minutes. Flip it to the other side and cook for 2 more minutes until it turns golden brown
7. Transfer to a plate and serve hot
8. You can also top it with fresh herbs and black pepper.

Rosemary flavored Potatoes

Servings: 4

Ingredients:

- 1 tablespoon rosemary (dried)
- 8 Yukon Gold potatoes (quartered)
- 1/4 cup olive oil
- 1 teaspoon pepper
- Salt to taste
- 1 teaspoon black pepper

Method:

1. Preheat the oven to 350 F.
2. Take a large bowl and place the quartered potatoes in it. Add the rosemary, pepper, olive oil and salt to the potatoes.
3. Toss them well to coat
4. Spread the coated potatoes evenly onto a cookie sheet.
5. Bake them in a preheated oven for 30 minutes until it turns golden brown
6. Transfer to a plate and sprinkle black pepper on it.
7. Serve warm

Millet Delight

Servings: 8

Ingredients:

- 1 cup millet (uncooked)
- 2/3 cup dates (chopped)
- 1/2 cup flaked coconut
- 1/2 cup soy milk powder
- 5 1/2 cups hot water
- 1 teaspoon vanilla extract

Method:

1. Preheat the oven to 350 F
2. Take a 9*13 inch casserole dish and combine the millet, dates, flaked coconut, soy milk powder, hot water and vanilla extract.
3. Use a spatula to combine them well.
4. Bake the casserole in a preheated oven for 30 minutes. Remove and stir.
5. Place the casserole back in the oven and bake for an additional 30 minutes
6. Transfer to a plate and serve hot

Akki Roti

Servings: 4

Ingredients:

- 1/2 cup green gram
- 1/4 cup carrot (shredded)
- 2 cups white rice flour
- 1/2 cup shredded coconut (unsweetened)
- 2 tablespoons fresh cilantro (finely chopped)
- 2 1/2 teaspoons chili pepper (finely chopped)
- 1/2 cup vegetable oil, divided
- 1/4 teaspoon asafoetida powder
- 1 teaspoon cumin seeds
- 1 cup water
- Salt to taste

Method:

1. Soak the green gram in water and refrigerate overnight.
2. Drain the grams the next day and grind them with a bit of water to form a smooth paste.
3. Mix the green gram, rice flour, chili pepper, cilantro, carrot, cumin seeds, asafetida, coconut and salt in a bowl.
4. Slowly add water and continue to mix with your hands until you get a dough consistency (be careful while adding water, the mixture shouldn't get too thin. 1/2 cup water should do).
5. Once the dough is ready, shape them into balls (size of a tennis ball). Flatten the ball and roll it into a thin circular form

6. Heat 2 tablespoons of vegetable oil on a skillet pan over medium heat.
7. Place the rolled dough (known as the roti) in the heated oil and fry for 40 seconds until it turns golden brown. Flip to the other side and fry for another 40 seconds until it turns golden brown.
8. Repeat steps 5 to 7 until you finish with the dough.
9. Transfer the akki roti to a plate and serve hot with ketchup or vegan butter

Veggie and Tofu scramble

Servings: 4

Ingredients:

- 14 ounces well-drained firm tofu
- 1 quartered tomato (large)
- 2 cups spinach leaves (lightly packed)
- 1/2 red onion (quartered)
- 1/2 yellow or red bell pepper (quartered)
- 3 garlic cloves
- 1/8 teaspoon sea salt (fine)

Method:

1. Combine the tomato, spinach, onion, bell pepper and garlic in a food processor and pulse until finely chopped.
2. Place the chopped vegetable mixture in a large skillet. Simmer over medium-high heat.
3. Add the tofu to the mixture and crumble it. Sprinkle the mixture with salt and cook as you continue to stir the contents.
4. Break if you find any large chunks of tofu while you cook.
5. Continue to cook for 8 minutes until the liquid has evaporated completely
6. Transfer to a plate and serve warm

Roasted Bell Pepper and Asparagus Tofu Frittata

Servings: 6

Ingredients:

- 1/2 block drained and crumbled firm tofu (14 ounces)
- 16 ounces drained silken tofu (1 package)
- 1/4 cup pitted and chopped Kalamata olives,
- 1 chopped leek (only the white and light green part)
- 1/2 cup chopped fresh basil (loosely packed)
- 1/2 cup roasted red bell peppers (chopped)
- 1/2 cup asparagus tips
- 1/2 cup light coconut milk (canned)
- 3 tablespoons nutritional yeast
- 1/4 teaspoon turmeric (ground)
- 2 tablespoons cornstarch
- 1/4 teaspoon black pepper (ground)
- 1 tablespoon tahini

Method:

1. Preheat the oven to 400. Take a 10-inch ovenproof nonstick skillet and fit a round-shaped parchment into it.
2. Blend the silken tofu, coconut milk, nutritional yeast, turmeric, cornstarch, black pepper and tahini in a food processor or blender until you get a puree consistency. Set this aside.
3. Preheat a large skillet over medium heat and add the leeks into it. Cook for 5 minutes until it begins to turn brown and stick to the skillet.

4. Add a splash of water and stir to dissolve the browned bits. Now add the crumbled firm tofu, red peppers, olives and asparagus into the skillet.

5. Cook for 5 minutes until the vegetables soften. Keep stirring often to prevent the contents getting burnt

6. Take a large bowl and combine the cooked vegetable mixture and pureed tofu. Mix well and add basil.

7. Pour this mix in a nonstick pan and bake in the oven for 20 minutes.

8. Remove the pan and run a rubber spatula or knife around the edges to prevent sticking.

9. Return it back to the oven and back for another 15 minutes until it becomes firm and turns golden

10. Once done, remove from the oven and let it sit for 10 minutes

11. Slice the frittata and transfer to a plate.

12. Serve warm and enjoy

Brunch Bread Pudding

Servings: 8

Ingredients:

- 6 cups cubed whole grain bread
- 1 pound silken tofu (1 package)
- 6 ounces smoky tempeh strips (crumbled into chunks or cut)
- 1/2 cup mixed chopped fresh herbs (parsley, thyme and chives)
- 1/3 cup flaxseed meal
- 1 pound trimmed and diagonally-sliced asparagus (divided)
- 3 cups almond milk (unsweetened)
- 1/4 teaspoon sea salt (fine)
- Canola spray oil
- 1/4 teaspoon black pepper (ground)

Method:

1. Preheat the oven to 350 F.
2. Spray a 9*13-inch casserole dish with canola spray oil.
3. Blend the tofu, flaxseed, almond milk, salt and pepper in a high-speed blender until it forms a smooth puree.
4. Toss together the bread, tempeh, 3/4 cup asparagus and salt in the prepared dish.
5. Pour the tofu puree over the top of the tossed bread and press gently to submerge all the bread pieces.
6. Scatter the remaining asparagus over the top and bake for 55 minutes

7. The pudding should be firm in the middle and turn golden brown on the top.
8. Remove from oven and let it cool for few minutes.
9. Transfer to a plate and serve warm

Chapter Four: Vegan Breakfast Sandwich Recipes

Balsamic Berry Grilled Cheese

Servings: 2

Ingredients:

- 1 cup sliced strawberries
- 1 tablespoon balsamic vinaigrette
- 1 cup blueberries
- 2 cups spinach
- 1 1/2 tablespoon coconut sugar
- 1 cup vegan mozzarella cheese shreds
- 2 teaspoons vegan butter (1 teaspoon per slice)
- Salt and pepper to taste
- Wheat brown bread (or any vegan bread of your choice)

Method:

1. Heat a saucepan over medium heat and place the blueberries in it.
2. Add the sliced strawberries, balsamic vinegar and coconut sugar into the saucepan
3. Allow the contents to boil as you stir the mixture gently.
4. Smash the berries while you stir and continue cooking
5. Once cooked, remove the berry mixture and transfer it to a strainer (keep a bowl underneath to collect the juice – you can use it for salad dressing if you like)

6. Spread 1 teaspoon of vegan butter on a slice of bread. The spread should be on the side you will be grilling or frying
7. Place the berry mixture, cheese shreds, spinach, cheese again, salt and pepper on the bread.
8. Take another bread slice and spread the remaining vegan butter on it. Place the bread on top of the other bread
9. Grill or fry on both sides for 2 minutes until it turns golden and crisp on the edges.
10. Repeat until you finish the berry mixture.
11. Transfer to a plate and enjoy.

Vegan Lox Bagel Sandwich

Servings: 2

Ingredients:

For the Vegan Lox

- 3 large carrots (wash and remove the skin)
- 2 nori sheets (broken into bits)
- 2 teaspoons vegan Worcestershire sauce
- 1 tablespoon soy sauce
- 1 teaspoon liquid smoke
- 1 tablespoon olive oil
- 1 cup water

For the Bagel Sandwich

- 2 Sprouted Wheat Bagels
- 1/2 thinly sliced red onion
- 1 Roma tomato (sliced)
- Capers, as needed
- Vegan cream cheese
- Fresh dill
- Salt and pepper

Method:

1. Preheat the oven to 400 degrees F
2. Brush the carrots with olive and place them on a baking tray
3. Bake the carrots for 30 minutes until it becomes soft and fragrant

4. Take a small bowl and combine the Worcestershire sauce, liquid smoke, nori sheet bits, vegan sauce and water

5. Whisk the contents together until well-combined and transfer to a shallow dish

6. Slice the baked carrots into thin strips (you can use a vegetable peeler)

7. Place the carrot strips in the marinade such that they are completely submerged.

8. Cover the shallow dish and refrigerate for 30 minutes to 1 hour (you can also do this the previous night)

9. Slice the wheat bagels into half and toast lightly. Now, spread the cream cheese on the slices.

10. Place the sliced tomatoes, carrot lox, fresh dill, carrot lox and capers. You can add more cheese if you like. Place the other slice on it.

11. Serve immediately.

Vegan Waffle Breakfast Sandwich

Servings: 4

Ingredients:

- 1/2 package extra-firm tofu (14-ounce – 1 package)
- 1/4 cup vegan cashew cheese
- 4 slices vegan bacon (you can get it from the store or make your own vegan bacon using tempeh or eggplant)
- 1 cup spinach
- 8 Root Veggie Hash Browns (you can get Dr. Praeger's)
- 1/4 teaspoon black pepper
- 1 sliced small tomato
- 1/2 teaspoon garlic powder
- 1 teaspoon ground turmeric
- 1/2 teaspoon onion powder
- 1/2 teaspoon black salt
- Non-stick cooking spray

Method:

1. Drain the tofu by pressing out the water for at least 20 minutes (you can use a tofu press). If you don't have a tofu press, wrap the tofu with some paper towels and place it on a shallow plate or in the sink. Place a heavy object on it (maybe a large pot with a weight inside) to press the water out.
2. Slice the tofu into four pieces (even) and set it aside

3. Mix the turmeric, onion powder, salt, garlic powder, pepper and 1/4 cup water in a small bowl. Stir until it combines well

4. Add the sliced tofu to the bowl and coat it with the mixture

5. Grease a skillet with cooking spray and place it over medium heat.

6. Add the coated tofu and cook for 7 minutes until brown and crispy. Flip and repeat

7. Grease a waffle iron lightly and add the hash browns to it (thaw the frozen hash browns before you add it to the waffle iron). Close the iron (make sure you add as many hash browns as possible)

8. Cook for 5 minutes and repeat for the remaining hash browns

9. Place the cooked hash browns on a baking sheet and keep it under the broiler for 7 minutes on low.

10. Wait until the hash browns are firm and crispy. Set it aside

11. Get the vegan bacon ready by cooking it according to the directions given in the package. Slice them into half and set aside.

12. Take a place and place 2 hash browns, add the spinach, tomato slice, tofu slice, 2 vegan bacon slices and 1 tablespoon of cashew cheese. Serve and enjoy!

Caribbean Black Bean with Jamaican Jerk Jackfruit Mango Sandwich

Servings: 4

Ingredients:

For the Jamaican Jerk Jackfruit:

- 20-ounce can young green jackfruit (1 can)
- 1 teaspoon parsley
- 1 teaspoon onion powder
- 2 teaspoons olive oil, divided
- 1.5 teaspoons garlic powder
- 1 teaspoon thyme
- 1 teaspoon paprika
- 1/4 teaspoon black pepper
- 3/4 teaspoon cayenne
- 2 cups water
- 1/4 teaspoon sugar
- 1 teaspoon lime juice
- 1/2 teaspoon salt

For the Caribbean Black Beans:

- 1.5 cups cooked black beans
- 2 finely chopped garlic cloves
- 1/2 cup onion (chopped)
- 1.5 tablespoons orange juice
- 1/4 teaspoon cayenne
- 1/4 teaspoon all spice powder
- 1/4 cup water
- 1/2 teaspoon thyme
- 1 teaspoon oil

- Pinch of salt

Other additions:

- Sliced cucumbers
- Chopped mango
- Toasted whole wheat bread slices
- Chopped cilantro
- Salt, pepper, lemon juice (to taste)
- 2 teaspoons vegan butter

Method:

Jamaican Jerk Jackfruit

1. Drain and wash the jackfruit. Use a paper napkin to squeeze out the water in the pieces and shred it using a food processor
2. Heat one teaspoon olive oil over medium heat in a skillet and add the shredded jackfruit to it
3. Add the onion powder, garlic powder, thyme, paprika, pepper, cayenne and salt to the skillet
4. Cook for 3 minutes until you get the roasted smell of the spices
5. Add the sugar, water and lime juice and cook for 30 minutes partially covering the skillet
6. Stir the mixture occasionally, as it turns dry. Add 1 teaspoon of oil and continue roasting the jackfruit until it turns golden brown on the edges. Sprinkle parsley.
7. Remove from heat and set it aside

Caribbean black beans

8. Heat oil over medium heat in a skillet and add the onions to it
9. Add the garlic and cook until the onions turn translucent and garlic gives the flavor
10. Add the black beans, orange juice, cayenne, spice powder, thyme and water. Let the contents simmer for 10 minutes as you continue stirring occasionally
11. Once cooked, remove from heat

Prepare the sandwich

12. Spread a teaspoon of vegan butter on the toasted bread slice.
13. Layer the black beans, chopped cilantro, jerk jackfruit, cucumber slices, mango slices, salt, pepper and a bit of lemon juice on the slice
14. Place another toasted slice and serve!

Spicy Blackened Chickpea Scramble Sandwich

Servings: 2

Ingredients:

- Toasted bread slices

For the blackening spice blend

- 1/2 teaspoon paprika
- 1/2 teaspoon coriander powder
- 1/2 teaspoon thyme
- 1/4 teaspoon cumin powder
- 1/4 teaspoon onion powder
- 1/4 teaspoon cayenne
- 1/2 teaspoon garlic powder
- Dash of white pepper
- Dash of black pepper

For the scramble

- 1.5 cups cooked Chickpeas
- 1/4 cup thinly sliced red onions
- Blackening spice blend (from above)
- 1/2 red bell pepper
- 1/2 tsp salt
- 1 tablespoon canola oil

Method:

1. Mix paprika coriander, thyme, cumin, onion powder, cayenne, garlic powder and a generous dash of white

and black pepper in a small bowl. Keep the spice blend aside

2. Toss the cooked chickpeas in the prepared blackening spice blend and let it sit
3. Heat the canola oil over high heat in a large skillet. Add the onion and bell pepper and cook until the contents are brown
4. Add the tossed chickpeas, the remaining spice powder from the bowl and salt to the onion-bell pepper mixture
5. Add a teaspoon of water to the spice powder bowl and add it to the skillet. Stir the contents thoroughly until well combined
6. Allow it to cook on high heat for 5 minutes as you continue to stir frequently to avoid the contents getting burnt (smash the contents while you stir)
7. Continue cooking until you smell the spices smoking (paprika and cayenne will begin to burn)
8. Remove from heat and a tablespoon of water to the scramble to add some moisture
9. Place the scramble on the toasted bread slice and serve.

Savory Tempeh Breakfast Sandwich

Servings: 2

Ingredients:

- 1 package tempeh (8 ounces)
- 3 split and toasted vegan English muffins (Trader Joe's British Muffins brand)
- 1/2 cup baby spinach
- 1/2 sliced avocado
- 3 tablespoons soy sauce
- 1 minced garlic clove,
- 1 1/2 tablespoons maple syrup
- 1 teaspoon smoked paprika
- 1 tablespoons apple cider vinegar
- 1 tablespoon olive oil
- 3/4 teaspoons black pepper
- Dijon mustard
- Ketchup

Method:

1. Combine the maple syrup, garlic, pepper, paprika, vinegar and soy sauce in a small bowl. Whisk them together.
2. Slice the tempeh into thick slabs – you may get 5-6 slabs in total
3. Heat olive oil over medium-high heat in a large skillet and add the tempeh slabs to the hot oil.
4. Spread the slaps in even layer and cook for 3 minutes until the bottom part is browned.

5. Pour the soy sauce mixture over the tempeh and cook for one more minute until the sauce dries up

6. The sauce will form a thick coating on the tempeh. Flip the tempeh slabs and cook for another 3 minutes until browned (by now the liquid would have cooked off completely). Remove from heat and set aside

7. Spread the ketchup and Dijon over the muffins quite liberally. Stuff it with the tempeh slabs.

8. Top it with baby spinach and avocado slices.

9. Serve and enjoy!

Vegan pesto Caprese sandwich

Servings: 4

Ingredients:

For the Vegan pesto

- 1/2 cup walnuts
- 2 cups basil leaves
- 2 garlic cloves
- 2 tablespoons olive oil
- 3 tablespoons nutritional yeast
- 1/2 teaspoon sea salt
- 2 tablespoons lemon juice

For the Vegan Mozzarella

- 2 tablespoons tapioca starch
- 1 teaspoon nutritional yeast
- 1/4 cup raw cashews (Soaked for 2 hours)
- 1 cup hot water
- 1 teaspoon olive oil
- 2 teaspoon lemon juice
- 1/2 teaspoon sea salt

For the sandwich

- 1 cup basil leaves
- 4 Roma tomatoes (sliced)
- Bread of choice

Method:

1. Get the vegan pesto ready first. Blend the walnuts, basil and garlic in a food processor. Add the salt, yeast

and lemon juice to the mixture and pulse again until well combined. As the food processor is running, slowly add the olive oil little at a time for the pesto to thin out. Once the pesto is smoothly blended, set it aside (you can also refrigerate to thicken for an easier spreading)

2. Blend the tapioca starch, yeast, soaked cashews (drain and wash once), olive oil, lemon juice, salt and water in a high-speed blender for 60 seconds until smooth and creamy

3. Heat this blended mixture over medium-high heat in a skillet and stir continuously with a wooden spoon.

4. Within minutes, the mixture will look like it is separating. Continue to mix it for 5 minutes until it thickens into a stretchy consistency (mozzarella-like). Set it aside

5. Divide the bread into 4 sandwiches and place the basil leaves on the bottom slice. Top it with mozzarella (you may have to chop the prepared mozzarella to pieces first) and then layer it with tomato slices. Add dollops of pesto and repeat the layers.

6. Serve and enjoy!

Chapter Five: Vegan Breakfast Savory Recipes

Shakshuka

Servings: 2

Ingredients:

- 1 block (12 ounces) unpressed medium tofu (cut into rounds)
- 3 cups diced tomatoes
- 4 large garlic cloves (peeled)
- 1/2 teaspoon dried chili flakes
- 1 teaspoon sugar
- 2 teaspoons dried herbs
- 1 tablespoon olive oil
- 1 teaspoon salt
- 1/2 teaspoon pepper

Method:

1. Heat the olive oil over medium heat in a skillet and add the garlic cloves. Cook for few seconds until the garlic turns slightly brown
2. Add the diced tomatoes, sugar, herbs, pepper, salt and black pepper to the skillet (*you can avoid the chili flakes if you don't want your dish to be too spicy*)
3. Simmer the contents for five minutes over medium heat
4. Now, add the tofu and reduce the heat to medium-low. Let it simmer for 15 minutes until the liquid thickens up a little.
5. The tofu becomes soft, continue to heat through and stir once more.

6. Once cooked, transfer to a plate and serve with toast or baguette
7. Enjoy!

Vegan Mushroom Spinach Omelet

Servings: 2

Ingredients:

For the Omelet

- 1 cup chickpea flour
- 1/2 teaspoon onion powder
- 3 tablespoons nutritional yeast
- 1/2 teaspoon garlic powder
- 1/2 teaspoon turmeric powder
- 1/4 teaspoon black salt
- 2 teaspoons olive oil
- 1/4 teaspoon sea salt
- 1 cup water

For the Filling

- 5 ounces coarsely chopped baby spinach
- 2 cups sliced mushrooms
- 1/4 cup diced onion
- 1 teaspoon olive oil
- Pinch of sea salt

For the Cheese Sauce

- 1/2 medium tomato (chopped)
- 1/2 cup raw cashews (soaked for two hours and drained)
- 2 teaspoons raw sesame seeds
- 1/2 teaspoon onion powder
- 2 tablespoons nutritional yeast
- 1/2 teaspoon garlic powder

- 1/4 teaspoon sea salt
- 2 tablespoons water
- 1 tablespoons lemon juice

For Serving
- 1/4 cup diced tomatoes
- 1/4 cup flat leaf parsley (chopped)

Method:

1. Take a medium bowl and combine the chickpea flour, onion powder, yeast, garlic powder, turmeric powder, olive oil, salt and water.
2. Whisk the contents together until well combined and let it sit for 10 minutes
3. Heat the olive oil over medium-high heat in a large skillet and add the onions to make the filling
4. Cook for 5 minutes until the onions turn brown.
5. Add the mushrooms now and sprinkle over with a pinch of salt. Mix well until the contents are combined thoroughly
6. Let it cook for some time until the mushrooms turn brown. Now, add the spinach and stir well. Cook until the leaves wilt and then cover the skillet. Transfer the contents to a bowl and set aside.
7. Heat the same skillet over medium-high heat and pour half of the prepared chickpea batter into it. Heat (since the skillet already has oil in it, you don't need to add more, but if the batter sticks to the bottom, you can add 1/4 teaspoon of oil)
8. Cook for 5 minutes until the edges begin to brown and the center bubbles lightly.

9. Flip it over gently and cook for another 3 minutes. Slide the omelet to a plate and cook the remaining batter in the same way

10. Blend the tomato, cashews, sesame seeds, onion powder, yeast, garlic powder, salt, water and lemon juice in a high-speed blender until you get thick consistency (like a sauce)

11. Layer the mushroom-spinach filling over the chickpea omelet (in the half part) and fold the omelet. Drizzle the cheese sauce over and top with chopped parsley and sliced tomatoes.

12. Repeat step 11 with the other chickpea omelet and serve hot. Enjoy!

Potato Leek Vegan Quiche

Servings: 6

Ingredients:

- 1 package drained extra-firm tofu (14 ounces)
- 1 cup diced Russet potato
- 1 medium leek, cleaned and chopped
- 2 tablespoons almond milk (unflavored)
- 2 tablespoons nutritional yeast flakes
- 2 minced garlic cloves
- 2 tablespoons soy sauce
- 1/4 teaspoon ground turmeric
- 1 vegan pie crust
- 1 tablespoon lemon juice
- 1 tablespoon olive oil
- Salt and pepper, to taste

Method:

1. Blend the tofu, yeast flakes, soy sauce, turmeric powder and lemon juice in a high-speed blender on high for 30 seconds until smooth and creamy. If the mixture is too thick, add a splash of milk and blend again.
2. Heat the oil in a large skillet over medium heat.
3. Add the diced potato when the oil is hot. Sprinkle salt and pepper over the potatoes and let it cook for 10 minutes until it softens. Flip the potatoes once in a while to ensure all the sides are cooked

4. Add the chopped leek and cook for 5 more minutes until the leeks soften. By now the potatoes would have turned crispy on the outside and become fork tender.
5. Add the minced garlic to the mixture and cook for a minute until the fragrance blends over.
6. Once the contents are cooked, turn off the heat and let it cool.
7. Now add the tofu blend to the potato-leek mixture in the skillet and mix well until well incorporated.
8. Preheat the oven to 375 degrees F
9. Fill the piecrust with this tofu-potato-leek mixture and smooth out the top with the back of a spoon or a spatula.
10. Bake the filled crust for 35 minutes until the crust edges turn brown and the center is set.
11. Once baked, let it sit for 15 minutes and then cut into slices as desired.
12. Serve and enjoy!

Easy Tofu Scramble with Mushrooms

Servings: 3

Ingredients:

- 1 1/2 cups sliced mushrooms
- 1 pound drained and pressed extra-firm tofu
- 1/2 cup cherry tomatoes (cut into half)
- 1/4 onion (diced)
- 2 teaspoons dried parsley
- 1 minced garlic clove
- 1/2 teaspoon dry mustard
- 1/4 teaspoon cumin
- 1/2 teaspoon smoked paprika
- 1/4 teaspoon turmeric
- 1/2 teaspoon salt
- 1/8 teaspoon pepper

Method:

1. Heat a skillet over medium heat and add 1-tablespoon water (I like oil-free but if you want you can add 1 tablespoon of oil instead of water).
2. Add onion and garlic to the skillet. Sauté the contents for 4 minutes until they become soft.
3. Add the mushroom to the onion-garlic mixture and continue to sauté until the contents reduce in volume.
4. Crumble the tofu into the contents in the skillet and mix well.
5. Add the parsley, mustard, cumin, paprika, turmeric, pepper and salt to the contents. Stir well until combined and continue to cook for 5 more minutes until the flavors blend completely.

6. Remove from heat and add the tomatoes now. Stir once more until the combined thoroughly
7. Transfer to a plate and serve hot

Turnip-Chickpea-Sweet Potato Hash

Servings: 2

Ingredients:

- 12 ounces peeled and sliced turnips (should be sliced to 0.5 inches)
- 1/2 cup cooked chickpeas (should be soaked overnight, then cooked until just tender for an hour and drained)
- 12 ounces peeled and sliced sweet potato (should be sliced to 0.5 inches)
- 1 chopped onion
- 1 deseeded and finely chopped red chili
- 2 finely chopped garlic cloves
- 2 tablespoons extra-virgin olive oil
- 1/2 teaspoon smoked paprika
- 1 tablespoon chopped fresh parsley
- 1/2 teaspoon dried oregano
- 1 tablespoon lemon juice
- 1/2 teaspoon sea salt

Method:

1. Heat the olive oil in a skillet over medium heat. Add the onion to the hot oil and stir-fry for 5 minutes until translucent and soft
2. Add the sweet potato, chili, turnip and garlic to the skillet. Stir well until combined
3. Add 2 tablespoons of water and reduce the heat to low flame. Cover the skillet and let it cook for 25 minutes.

Stir frequently until the vegetables become tender and turn light brown.

4. Now add the cooked chickpeas, oregano, smoked paprika and salt to the veggies. Let it cook for 5 more minutes as you continue stirring often. (You don't need to cover the skillet this time)

5. Once the contents in the skillet are completely cooked, remove from heat and add the lemon juice.

6. Sprinkle the chopped parsley over the cooked chickpea-potato-turnip hash.

7. Transfer to a plate and serve hot!

Gluten-Free Vegan Cauliflower Hash Browns

Servings: 6 patties

Ingredients:

- 1/2 cauliflower head (break into florets)
- 1/4 cup chickpea flour
- 1 tablespoon cornstarch or arrowroot starch
- 1/2 onion (chopped)
- 1/2 teaspoon garlic powder
- 1 tablespoon coconut oil
- 1/2 teaspoon salt
- 2 tablespoons water

Method:

1. Preheat oven to 400 degrees F
2. Grease the baking sheet with coconut oil and set aside
3. Pulse the cauliflower florets and chopped onion in a food processor until crumbly. You can also grate it with a box grater until you get the crumbles.
4. Take a large bowl and place the cauliflower-onion mixture in it.
5. Add the cornstarch, chickpea flour, salt, garlic powder and water to it. Stir well until combined thoroughly.
6. The batter should be in a thick consistency so that you can comfortably make patties with it.
7. Divide it into 6 equal portions and shape them into 3x2 inches patties.

8. Place the patties on the greased baking sheet and bake for 40 minutes until it turns golden brown (flip it halfway through the baking process)
9. Transfer to a plate and serve warm.

Jicama Fries

Servings: 1 1/2 cup

Ingredients:

- 1 cup peeled and diced jicama (1/2 jicama should do)
- 1/4 red onion (minced)
- 1/2 red bell pepper (diced)
- 1/2 teaspoon garlic powder
- 1/2 green bell pepper (diced)
- 1/2 teaspoon onion powder
- 1/4 teaspoon sea salt
- 1/2 teaspoon smoked paprika
- 1 tablespoon +1 teaspoon olive oil
- 1 tablespoon water

Method:

1. Heat olive oil in a skillet over medium heat. Add the diced jicama and sauté for 2 minutes.
2. Add 1-tablespoon water to the sautéed jicama and cover the skillet with a lid.
3. Let it continue to cook over medium heat for 7 minutes until it softens
4. Remove the lid and 1 teaspoon of oil to the skillet. Add the onions and bell peppers to the jicama.
5. Sauté the contents for 5 minutes until jicama turns light brown
6. Add the onion powder, paprika, garlic powder and salt to the continents. Mix well until combined thoroughly
7. Continue to sauté until all the contents are browned
8. Transfer to a plate and serve hot!

Cheesy Vegan Breakfast Potato Casserole

Servings: 8

Ingredients:

- 3 medium potatoes (diced)
- 1 medium onion (finely chopped)
- 14 ounces vegan Italian sausage (crumbled or thinly sliced)
- 1/2 teaspoon red pepper flakes
- 3 minced garlic cloves
- 1 teaspoon olive oil
- 2 tablespoons + 1 teaspoon chopped parsley
- Salt to taste

For the cheesy sauce:
- 3/4 cup raw cashews (soaked for 30 minutes in 1 1/2 cups water)
- 1/2 teaspoon dry sage
- 2 teaspoons onion powder
- 1/4 cup nutritional yeast
- 1 teaspoon garlic powder
- Salt and ground black pepper, to taste

Method:

1. Blend the soaked cashews (wash it with water and drain), dry sage, onion powder, yeast, garlic powder, salt and pepper in a high-speed blender for 60 seconds until creamy and smooth. Set the cheesy sauce aside

2. Take a microwave-safe dish and place the potatoes in it. Add 1 tablespoon of water and cover the dish. Microwave on high for five minutes until the potatoes are soft and tender

3. Heat the oil in a cast-iron skillet (10-inch should be good) and add the onions, parsley and garlic to the hot oil. (*You can also use any skillet that can comfortably go from stove to oven*)

4. Sprinkle the contents with salt and pepper. Sauté over medium heat for five minutes until the onions turn soft and translucent.

5. Add the cooked potatoes and sausage to the onion mixture. Stir well until combined and let it cook for 5 minutes. Add more salt and pepper if required (you can taste and check)

6. Spread the potato mixture evenly in the skillet and pour the cheesy sauce over it. Be generous and ensure you have the potato completely covered with the sauce evenly.

7. Place the skillet in the oven and bake for 30 minutes until the top part turns light brown and you can see gold-brown spots on the potatoes and the sauce

8. Remove from oven and garnish with 1-teaspoon parsley.

9. Serve hot and enjoy!

Note: You can also transfer the cooked potato mixture from the skillet to a greased baking tray and then bake it in the oven!

Savory Veggie Quinoa Flakes

Servings: 1

Ingredients:

- 1/3 cup quinoa flakes
- 1/4 cup zucchini (shredded)
- A handful of torn baby spinach
- 1/4 teaspoon smoked paprika
- 1 tablespoon nutritional yeast
- 1 tablespoon hemp seeds
- 1/4 teaspoon turmeric powder
- 1/4 teaspoon onion powder
- 1/8 teaspoon cumin powder
- 2/3 Cup + 2 tablespoons Water

Method:

1. Take a big microwave safe bowl and combine the quinoa flakes, paprika, yeast, hemp seeds, turmeric powder, onion powder and cumin powder. Mix well until combined
2. Add the shredded zucchini, spinach and water to the bowl. Mix until the flavors blend and the contents are incorporated well.
3. Place the bowl in the microwave and cook on high for 2 minutes
4. Carefully remove the bowl and serve hot.

Chapter Six: Vegan Breakfast Taco Recipes

Vegan Spicy Scrambled Tofu Breakfast Tacos

Servings: 3

Ingredients:

For the spicy scrambled tofu

- 1 block sprouted firm (16-ounce)
- 3 Roma tomatoes
- 1/2 cup roasted red bell pepper (chopped)
- 1/2 medium red onion (diced)
- 1 cored and diced poblano pepper
- 1 tablespoon smoked paprika
- 1 tablespoon chili powder
- 1/2 tablespoon extra-virgin olive oil
- 3/4 teaspoon sea salt
- Juice of 1 lime

For the base and toppings

- 1 pitted and peeled ripe avocado (slice into half and mash it with sea salt and lime juice)
- 10 small corn tortillas (warmed)
- Cilantro leaves

Method:

1. Heat olive oil in a large skillet over medium heat. Add the red onion and poblano pepper to the hot oil.

2. Sauté for 6 minutes until they begin to soften. Keep stirring occasionally to prevent the contents from burning

3. Blend the Roma tomatoes in a high-speed blender until it gets the puree form (not the complete puree but with bits of tomato pieces in it). Set the tomato puree aside.

4. Add the chili powder, roasted red pepper, salt and smoked paprika to the onion-pepper mixture. Saute for another minute until the spices blend and become fragrant

5. Add the tomato puree to the mixture and stir well. Crumble the tofu to the contents in the skillet and mix well until combined

6. Simmer for 12 minutes until the liquid evaporates as you continue to stir occasionally

7. Add the lime juice and simmer for one more minute. Remove from heat and season it again with salt (based on your desired taste)

8. Take the warm tortilla and place the scrambled tofu filling on it.

9. Top with mashed avocado and cilantro leaves.

10. Serve immediately

Mexican Vegan Taco

Servings: 6

Ingredients:

- 6 corn tortillas
- 10 ounces firm tofu
- 15 ounces cooked or canned black beans
- 1/2 red bell pepper (chopped)
- 1/2 red onion (chopped)
- 1/2 green bell pepper (chopped)
- 1 avocado (sliced)
- 1/4 teaspoon turmeric powder
- Ground black pepper, to taste
- 1/4 teaspoon sea salt
- Salsa to taste

Method:

1. Preheat oven to 400 degrees F.
2. Cover 2 rows of the oven rack with the corn tortillas and bake them for 10 minutes until it turns golden brown. Set it aside.
3. Sauté the onion, green bell pepper and red bell pepper in a skillet with 2 tablespoons of water over medium-high heat for 5 minutes until they are cooked. (You can replace water with oil if you desire)
4. Stir occasionally and continue to cook the veggies. Set them aside once done.
5. Crumble the tofu in a pan; add salt and turmeric powder with some water.
6. Stir and cook for 5 minutes over medium-high heat until the tofu is cooked well. Set this aside.

7. If you are using canned black beans, drain and rinse them. Reheat the drained beans in a frying pan with some water (*if you are using cooked black beans, you can directly add it to the taco*)

To assemble the tacos

8. Place the tofu scramble on the baked corn tortillas; top it with the black beans, cooked veggies (onion-bell pepper), salsa and avocado slices.
9. Serve immediately and enjoy!

Fall Inspired Breakfast Tacos with Avocado Cream

Servings: 2 tacos

Ingredients:

- 4 corn tortillas
- 1/4 purple cabbage head (chopped)
- 2 cups thinly sliced mushrooms
- 1 medium delicata squash
- Fresh cilantro (handful)
- 1 tin black beans
- 3 thinly sliced garlic cloves
- 1 knob fresh ginger (peeled and grated)
- 3 tablespoons olive oil
- 1 teaspoon maple syrup
- 2 tablespoons lemon juice
- Sea salt, to taste

For the Avocado Cream
- 2 ripe avocados (peeled and deseeded)
- 1 large handful fresh cilantro + 1 teaspoon chopped cilantro (for garnishing)
- 1 heaping tablespoon Vegan Dressing (Best Foods brand)
- Juice of 1/2 lemon
- Sea salt

Method:

1. Preheat oven to 420 degrees F

2. Cut the squash vertically from the center; remove the seed and pulp. Now, slice them into thin half-moon shapes.
3. Drizzle some olive oil and salt over the sliced squash. Mix them well.
4. Grease a baking sheet with parchment and place the oil-salt coated squash on it.
5. Bake for 30 minutes and flipping the squash halfway through as it gets cooked.
6. Meanwhile get the avocado sauce ready by blending the avocados, cilantro, vegan dressing and salt in a high-speed blender. Blend on high for 45 seconds until creamy and smooth
7. Heat 3 tablespoons olive oil over medium heat in a small pan. Add the ginger and garlic to the hot oil, sauté for 3 minutes until the raw smell goes
8. Add the mushrooms and cabbage to the ginger-garlic mixture and cook for 5 more minutes until the cabbage softens
9. Add the maple syrup and lemon juice to the pan, mix well until the contents are combined thoroughly
10. Sprinkle some salt and add the black beans to the mixture. Let it cook for 3 more minutes. Remove from heat and set aside
11. Warm the tortillas in a hot pan for 10-15 seconds on each side
12. Assemble the tacos by spreading a layer of avocado cream, the veggie mix (cabbage-mushroom-black beans), roasted squash (which would have been ready by now) and chopped cilantro.
13. Serve and enjoy!

Southwest breakfast tacos

Servings: 8 tacos

Ingredients:

- 8 Southwest Hash Browns (Dr. Praeger's brand)
- 16 ounces drained and pressed extra-firm tofu
- 1/2 cup white onion (chopped)
- 1 cup cooked black beans
- 8 flour tortillas
- 4 cups spinach leaves
- 1 can drained green chilies (4.5 ounces)
- 1 tablespoon olive oil
- 1/4 teaspoon black salt
- 1/2 teaspoon garlic powder
- 1/4 teaspoon black pepper (freshly ground)
- 1/4 teaspoon chili powder
- 1/2 teaspoon cumin powder
- 1/4 teaspoon turmeric
- Sliced avocado and hot sauce (for serving)

Method:

1. Preheat oven to 450 degrees F
2. Place the hash browns on the baking pan (ungreased) and bake for 5 minutes until they become brown. Flip and bake for another 4 minutes until heated through and browned. Remove from oven and set it aside.
3. Heat olive oil over medium heat in a large skillet and add the onion to it. Cook for 3 minutes until soft and translucent.

4. Crumble the tofu (drained and pressed) into pieces and add it to the onions in the skillet
5. Season it with black salt and other spices (garlic powder, black pepper, chili powder, cumin powder and turmeric).
6. Sauté the mixture for mixture for 4 minutes until browned and heated through
7. Add the cooked black beans, green chilies and spinach to the skillet. Cook for 5 more minutes until the spinach wilts
8. Add more salt and pepper if desired.
9. Place the tofu scramble on the tortilla, then the baked hash brown, avocado slice and hot sauce.
10. Serve and enjoy (repeat with the remaining tortillas)

Chapter Four: Vegan Breakfast Crepe & Pancake Recipes

Sweet Pancakes

Servings: 4

Ingredients:

- 4 cups self-rising flour
- 1 tablespoon custard powder
- 1 tablespoon white sugar
- 1/4 cup soy milk

Method:

1. Mix together the flour, custard powder and sugar in a large bowl until they combine well.
2. Add the soy milk to the mixture and whisk until there are no lumps
3. Heat a griddle over medium heat and coat it with nonstick cooking spray.
4. Take a spoon of the whisked batter and spread it onto the surface of the griddle.
5. Let it cook until bubbles start to form on the batter surface.
6. Use a spatula and flip the pancake to the other side. Let it cook until golden.
7. Transfer to a plate and serve warm.

Authentic Potato Pancakes

Servings: 10

Ingredients:

- 10 peeled and shredded russet potatoes
- 1 finely diced onion
- 1 peeled and shredded carrot
- 5 crushed garlic cloves
- 2 cups dry breadcrumbs
- 1 tablespoon fresh dill (chopped)
- 1 tablespoon flat leaf parsley (chopped)
- 2 tablespoons all-purpose flour
- 1/4 cup olive oil
- 2 tablespoons lemon juice (fresh)
- Salt and pepper to taste

Method:

1. Mix the potatoes, onion, carrot, garlic, dill and parsley in a large bowl. Now, add the lemon juice, olive oil, breadcrumbs, flour, salt and pepper.
2. Mix well and knead with your hands until it holds together
3. Take a skillet and heat the olive oil over medium heat.
4. Drop a spoonful of potato mixture in the hot oil. Cook for 4 minutes until it turns golden brown. Flip to the other side and cook until it is crispy and golden brown
5. Transfer to a plate and serve hot

Crispy Vietnamese Crepes

Servings: 4 crepes

Ingredients:

For the batter

- 1 cup rice flour
- 1/2 cup coconut cream
- 1/2 cup cornstarch
- 2 teaspoons turmeric
- 2 cups water
- 1 teaspoon salt

For the nuoc charm

- 2 finely minced cloves garlic
- 1 tablespoon sugar
- 1/3 cup Fysh sauce
- Juice of one lime

For crepes

- 2 chopped scallions,
- 2 handfuls of bean sprouts
- 1 tablespoon canola oil
- 2 halved and thinly sliced shallots
- 2 thinly sliced king oyster mushroom stems
- 1/2 bunch brown beech mushrooms
- A handful of oyster mushrooms (remove the stems and chop roughly)

To serve

- A handful of fresh mint
- A handful of fresh basil

Method:

1. Mix the rice flour, cornstarch, water, coconut cream, turmeric and salt in a large bowl and refrigerate overnight.
2. Take a small bowl and combine the garlic, Fysh sauce, sugar and lime juice. Mix well until combined.
3. Heat 1 tablespoon canola oil in a skillet over medium heat. Add half scallions and shallots to the hot oil.
4. Stir-fry until golden and add half the brown beech mushrooms. Stir well until the flavors blend.
5. Pour one ladle of batter over the mushroom-scallion mixture in the pan. Spread evenly to coat the pan.
6. Sprinkle the bean sprouts, oyster mushrooms and king oyster over the top.
7. Cover the skillet with a lid, reduce the heat to medium low and let it cook for 3 minutes until crispy and the edges turn dry
8. Uncover and cook for 2 more minutes. Use a spatula to slide under the crepe and it would easily come off the bottom. Fold into half and transfer to a plate
9. Repeat until the batter is over.
10. Serve hot with nuoc cham and fresh herbs. Enjoy!

Simple Vegan Pancakes

Servings: 6

Ingredients:

- 1 cup organic whole wheat flour
- 1 cup almond milk
- 2 tablespoons + 1 teaspoon coconut oil (melted)
- 1 tablespoon baking powder
- 2 tablespoons maple syrup
- 1 teaspoon pure vanilla extract
- 1/4 teaspoon salt

Method:

1. Take a medium-sized bowl and combine the wheat flour, baking powder and salt. Mix well until combined

2. Take another bowl and whisk together the almond milk, 2 tablespoons melted coconut oil, maple syrup and vanilla extract. The mixture should be thoroughly melted. (In case the melted coconut oil solidifies when it comes in contact with the cold milk, warm it until it melts again – you can use a microwave)

3. Pour the milk mixture into the flour mixture and stir well until combined. It is ok if few lumps remain as over-mixing can give you hard pancakes. Let the batter sit for 5 minutes so that you get nice and fluffy pancakes.

4. Heat a heavy-bottomed cast iron skillet over medium-low heat. The surface should be hot enough for a drop of water to sizzle on contact

5. Grease the skillet with 1/4 teaspoon oil and scoop the pancake batter using a 1/4 cup measure onto the hot skillet

6. Cook on low heat until it becomes golden brown on both sides.

7. Repeat with the remaining batter and serve the pancakes warm.

Banana Oatmeal Quinoa Pancakes

Servings: 6

Ingredients:

- 1 7-inches long ripe banana
- 1/2 cup quick cooking oats (gluten-free)
- 1/4 cup rinsed and drained raw quinoa
- 1/2 cup coconut milk
- 1/2 cup all-purpose flour (gluten-free)
- 2 tablespoon + 1 teaspoon coconut oil
- 1 teaspoon baking powder
- 1/2 teaspoon pure stevia extract powder
- 1/2 teaspoon cinnamon powder
- 1/2 cup water

Method:

1. Pour 1/2 cup water into a saucepan and add the quinoa (rinsed and drained) to it. Heat the pan over high heat and bring the water to boil.
2. Reduce the heat to low, cover the saucepan and simmer for 10 minutes
3. Meanwhile, peel the banana and cut it. Mash the cut pieces using a fork or you can use the food processor too.
4. Pour the coconut milk into a small bowl. Add the mashed banana and 1 tablespoon oil to the milk. Beat the mixture well until thoroughly combined
5. Turn off the heat when the quinoa is half-cooked and let it cool for 5 minutes.
6. Take a large bowl and combine the gluten-free oats, half-cooked quinoa, gluten-free flour, baking powder,

stevia powder and cinnamon powder. Toss them together until the contents are well incorporated.

7. Pour the banana-milk mixture to the oats-flour-quinoa mixture. Mix the contents well until all the dry flour gets combined with the banana-milk mixture. Let the batter be of a consistency suitable for a pancake.

8. Heat a skillet or frying pan over medium heat and grease it with coconut oil.

9. Scoop the batter (measure 1 ice cream scoop) and drop it into the hot pan. Carefully spread the batter to 5 inches diameter using a rubber spatula.

10. Drop 2 more scoops and repeat step 9 (you can make 3 pancakes in the pan at the same time). Make sure the batter doesn't touch the other pancakes while making the round shape

11. Cover the pan and let it cook until it becomes golden brown on each side.

12. Transfer to a plate and serve warm!

Potato Latkes

Servings: 10 small pancakes

Ingredients:

- 1/4 cup all purpose flour
- 1 grated small onion,
- 2 big potatoes
- 1 teaspoon cumin powder
- 1/2 teaspoon chili powder
- 1 teaspoon coriander powder
- 2 tablespoons coconut oil
- 3 tablespoons coriander/cilantro (chopped)
- Salt, to taste

Method:

1. Peel the potatoes and wash them thoroughly. Grate the potatoes using a box grater and squeeze out the excess liquid from the grated potatoes
2. Transfer the grated potatoes to a large bowl and add the flour, grated onion, cumin powder, chili powder, coriander powder, chopped coriander and salt.
3. Mix them well without adding water, as the water content in the onion should be enough for the batter consistency.
4. Heat one tablespoon of oil in a large heavy bottomed skillet over medium heat.
5. Scoop a heaping tablespoon of batter and flatten it using your hand (grease your hands and place the batter on your palm and flatten it using the other hand).

6. Place the flattened batter gently on the hot oil. Repeat step 5 and make 3 or 4 potato pancakes and add it to the skillet (don't overcrowd the skillet).

7. Reduce the heat to low-medium heat and cook for 2 minutes until golden brown. Flip it to the other side and cook for another minute until it turns brown.

8. Repeat steps 5 to 7 with the remaining potato mixture.

9. Spread paper towels on a big plate and place the cooked potato pancakes on it (*this will help drain the excess oil onto the paper towels*)

10. Serve warm and enjoy!

Vegan Carrot Coconut Pancakes

Servings: 3

Ingredients:

- 1/2 cup carrot (finely grated)
- 1/4 cup finely shredded coconut, divided (unsweetened)
- 1 cup unbleached all-purpose flour
- 1 cup coconut or almond milk
- 1 heaping tablespoon melted non-dairy butter (Earth Balance brand)
- 2 tablespoons organic sugar
- 1 teaspoon pure vanilla extract
- 1 1/2 teaspoon baking powder
- Pinch of sea salt
- 2 tablespoons crushed walnuts or pecans
- 1 tablespoon coconut oil

Method:

1. Take a large bowl and combine 2 tablespoons shredded coconut, flour, sugar, baking powder and sea salt. Whisk together until thoroughly blended.
2. Pour the almond milk into another bowl and add the butter to it. Now, add the vanilla extract and whisk together until combined well.
3. Add the milk-butter mixture to the coconut-flour mixture and stir well until the contents blend well.
4. Add the shredded carrot and mix once again. Let the batter sit for 5 minutes for the pancakes to come soft and fluffy.

5. Heat a large iron skillet over medium heat and grease the surface with coconut oil
6. Scoop the batter using 1/4-cup measure and drop it on the hot skillet. Spread the batter a bit (should be small) and sprinkle the crushed walnuts and shredded coconut.
7. Cook for 2 minutes until the bubbles appear in the center part and the edges look dry. Flip it to the other side and cook for another minute.
8. Transfer to a plate and serve with non-dairy butter.

Spinach Pancakes

Servings: 12 pancakes

Ingredients:

- 3 cups fresh spinach
- 2/3 cup rice flour
- 3 tablespoons freshly ground flax seed
- 1 tablespoon baking powder
- 1/2 cup + 1 tablespoon warm water
- 1 teaspoon finely minced garlic
- Sea salt, for taste
- Non-stick cooking spray

Method:

1. Take a small bowl and combine the flax seed with 1-tablespoon warm water. Mix well and refrigerate for some time to form a gel-like consistency
2. Pulse the flaxseed gel and fresh spinach in a food processor until blended thoroughly.
3. Add the rice flour and baking powder to the flax-spinach mixture. Pulse again until completely blended. Add the remaining water and pulse for one last time.
4. Transfer the batter to a large bowl. Add the minced garlic and salt to the batter. Mix thoroughly until the contents are well-incorporated
5. Heat a nonstick griddle over low heat and grease it with the cooking spray

6. Pour the batter in 1/4-cup increments to the hot griddle and spread it to form a 3- inch pancake. You can make 4-6 pancakes in one shot.
7. Flip the pancake until cooked through and repeat with the remaining batter
8. Transfer the bright green spinach pancake to a plate and serve warm.

Vegan Apple Cinnamon Pancakes

Servings: 4

Ingredients:

- 1 cup Spelt flour
- 1/4 cup applesauce (unsweetened)
- 1/3 teaspoon cinnamon
- 1 cup almond milk
- 1 tablespoon baking powder
- 2 tablespoons melted vegan buttery spread+ more for greasing (Earth Balance brand)
- 1/2 teaspoon vanilla extract
- 1 1/2 tablespoons sugar
- 1/4 teaspoon salt

Method:

1. Take a small bowl and combine the spelt flour, cinnamon, baking powder, sugar and salt together. Use a fork to whisk together until mixed well
2. Pour the almond milk into another medium-sized bowl. Add the applesauce, 2 tablespoons melted buttery spread and vanilla extract to the milk. Whisk together until blended well.
3. Add the flour-cinnamon mixture to the milk-sauce mixture and stir well.
4. Let the batter sit for 5 minutes while you heat a large iron skillet over medium-high heat.
5. Add 1 tablespoon of buttery spread to the hot skillet and wait for it to melt

6. Reduce the heat to medium-low heat and spoon the batter onto the hot skillet. Spread a bit to form a nice round shape.
7. Cook for 2 minutes until the edges turn crispy and bubbles start forming in the center. Flip the pancake and cook for 1 more minute until it turns light brown.
8. Remove the pancake and transfer to a plate. Repeat steps 6 and 7 for the remaining batter.
9. Once done, serve warm and enjoy!

Vegan Triple Berry Sheet Pan Pancakes

Servings: 16 square pancakes

Ingredients:

- 1 cup chopped strawberries
- 1/2 cup raspberries
- 1 cup Blueberries
- 3 cups all purpose flour
- 3 cups almond milk
- 3 tablespoons baking powder
- 1 tablespoon apple cider vinegar
- 1/3 cup maple syrup
- 1 teaspoon salt
- 1/3 cup melted coconut oil
- 2 teaspoons vanilla
- 1 teaspoon Lemon zest
- Non-stick cooking spray

Method:

1. Preheat oven to 425 degrees F
2. Take a medium-sized bowl and combine the apple cider vinegar along with almond milk. Stir once and let it sit to thicken a bit
3. Take a large bowl and combine the all purpose flour, baking powder and salt. Whisk together to combine and set it aside.
4. Now, add the maple syrup, coconut oil and vanilla to the almond milk-vinegar mixture. Stir carefully
5. Add this mixture to the flour mixture and whisk well until thoroughly combined

6. Add 1 teaspoon lemon zest to the mixture and stir again.
7. Line an 11x16 inch-sheet pan with parchment paper and spray a bit of non-stick cooking spray.
8. Pour the entire batter here and smooth it out. Bake for 5 minutes and sprinkle the berries on top.
9. Rotate and bake for another 12 minutes until the pancake is completely baked. Prick it with a toothpick and see if it comes out clean
10. Broil for 4 minutes until it becomes brown (in case you don't want the browning to happen, skip this step)
11. Serve with maple syrup and enjoy!

Conclusion

I would like to take this opportunity to thank you once again for choosing this book.

An important thing to keep in mind is that a vegan diet doesn't mean a low fat or low-carb diet – it is not about cutting the macros but cutting the meat and dairy. You can find a lot of scientific and anecdotal evidence on the benefits of vegan diets, which is usually life-changing for an individual. You not only reduce your carbon footprint but also make your body feel healthier and lighter.

Veganism has the element of compassion, which not only spares the animals (irrespective of the *ethically raised meat* stamps) from suffering but also the humans who are forced to work in *not-so-humane* slaughterhouse conditions. You contribute the least to the side effects of large-scale meat production such as climate change, water wastage, deforestation and greenhouse gas emissions when you go vegan.

The book has covered the primary objective, which is to serve as a vegan breakfast cookbook for any health-conscious individual who doesn't want to compromise on his or her taste buds. The chapters concentrate on the numerous healthy homemade vegan breakfast recipes that include smoothies, soups, simple breakfast dishes and brunch items.

I sincerely hope this book was useful and has helped you decide a quick fix vegan breakfast option.

The healthy vegan recipes mentioned in the book are entirely plant-based which can serve as a well-balanced diet for you and your entire family. So, what are you waiting for? Try all the recipes mentioned in the book and start working towards an environment-friendly diet option.

Finally, if you enjoyed this book, then I'd like to ask you for a favor. Will you be kind enough to leave a review for this book on Amazon? It would be greatly appreciated!

Thank you and good luck!

Other Books by Grizzly Publishing

"Jamaican Cookbook: Traditional Jamaican Recipes Made Easy"

https://www.amazon.com/dp/B07B68KL8D

"Brazilian Instant Pot Cookbook: Delicious Pressure Cooked Meals Made Fast and Easy"

https://www.amazon.com/dp/B078XBYP89

"Norwegian Cookbook: Traditional Scandinavian Recipes Made Easy"

https://www.amazon.com/dp/B079M2W223

"Casserole Cookbook: Delicious Casserole Recipes From Around The World"

https://www.amazon.com/dp/B07B6GV61Q

Made in United States
Troutdale, OR
03/28/2024

18750383R00076